Koala Facts
For Kids

Copyright©2022HarmonyWells

While researching this book, I found an interesting video that exhibits some of the different sounds that koalas make. You can scan the barcode below to go to the video, or type in the web address to hear them.

https://www.youtube.com/watch?v=fq74aS4irmc

Koalas are not bears. They are marsupials (they carry their babies in a pouch as they develop.)

They are more closely related to kangaroos and wombats.

They are only found in the wild in southeastern and eastern Australia, Queensland, New South Wales, Victoria, and South Australia.

The male is called a buck, and the female a doe. Baby koalas are called joeys.

They live up high in eucalyptus trees.

They eat only eucalyptus leaves, which are poisonous to most animals.

A special digestive organ and bacteria help to detoxify the chemicals in the leaves.

Of over 700 species of eucalyptus, they will eat fewer than 50.

They eat an average of 1 pound of leaves daily.

Only about 25% of what they eat can be digested, which is why they need to eat a lot.

For extra minerals koalas will sometimes eat mud.

Because of their diet, the juveniles and females smell like eucalyptus, and the males just a little muskier.

The eucalyptus scent acts as a natural insect repellent.

They have poor vision, but excellent hearing and a great sense of smell.

Their arms and legs are very strong, and their claws are sharp.

Koalas can sleep up to 18 hours a day, because they don't get many nutrients from the eucalyptus leaves, and need to conserve their energy.

They have unique fingerprints (like humans and primates) and unique patterns on their noses.

They have 5 digits on each paw, two of them opposing like thumbs, so they can grip trees and food.

They have rough pads on their hands and feet, and their back feet have two toes fused together that they use for grooming.

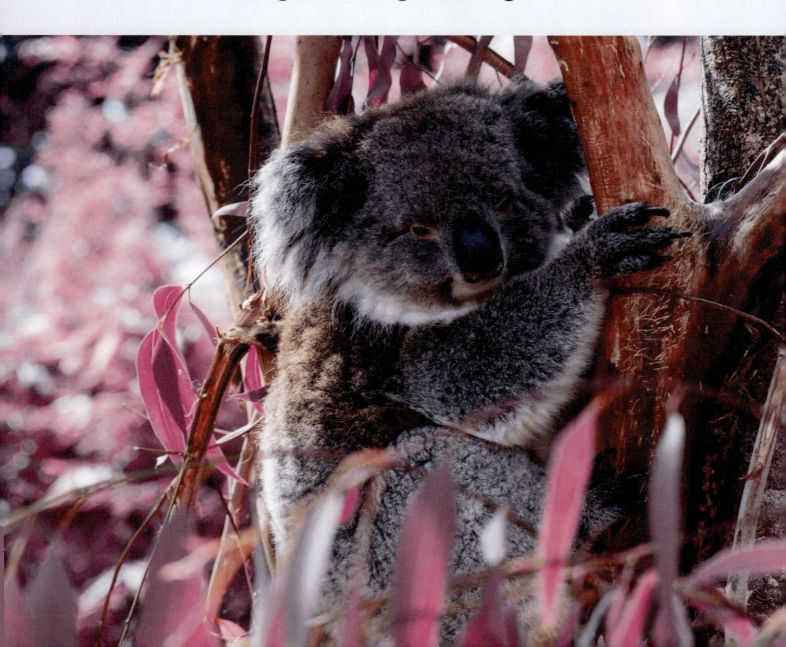

Koalas in southern Australia are larger, and have more fur than the koalas in the north. Their fur is more of a brownish color.

They are born deaf, blind, and with no fur. They are only the size of a peanut at birth.

When babies are born they are underdeveloped.

But they do have a developed sense of smell and touch, and a sense of direction.

The females are pregnant for just 35 days before the joey comes out and climbs into the pouch.

Babies develop in their mother's pouch for about six months.

Then they ride on their mom's back or stomach for another six months, during which time they still sleep and eat in the pouch.

Females will usually just have one joey every 1-3 years. The babies stay with their mother until another joey is born.

The word koala is said to mean "no water." They usually get all the water they need from the moisture in the leaves they eat.

They only come down to drink water in very hot or dry weather.

Thick fur and extra cartilage at the base of the spine makes sitting in tree branches all day more comfortable.

Males are up to 50% larger than females, and have a broader face and larger nose. They also have a large, dark scent gland on their chest.

The scent gland secretes a dark, sticky substance.

Males define their territory by rubbing their scent gland, and by making scratch marks on the trees.

Females have a clean white chest, and a backward (outward) facing pouch. The pouch prevents injury to the baby as mom is moving about in the trees.

Their fur is like the coarse wool of a sheep, not as soft and fuzzy as it looks.

Their weight can range from 11 pounds to 26 pounds depending on gender and location.

They have 2 sets of vocal chords allowing them to make a variety of sounds. They often communicate with grunting or wailing sounds.

But they can make a range of noises, including a bellow that sounds like a loud snore and then a belch.

They are solitary. Females usually stay in the same area where they were born, while the males are travelers, and establish their own territories.

The territories vary in size based on gender, age, and social position, as well as the quality of the habitat.

On the ground they usually move slowly, as they are not adapted to walking on the ground.

When disturbed they can move as fast as about 18 miles per hour.

They are nocturnal, meaning they are most active at night.

Their average lifespan in the wild is about 10-12 years.

Unlike other marsupials, koalas have no tail.

Koala fossils have been found in Australia that date back about 20 million years.

They have a small brain for a mammal of their size.

In 2006 thieves tried to steal a Koala from a zoo, but found it too cranky, and stole a crocodile instead.

May 3rd has been named "Wild Koala Day."

Due to wildfires and loss of habitat, koalas are now considered endangered.

Printed in Great Britain
by Amazon